Modern slavery

FULL ALERT

KO6 Editions

A CALL From the Author

To: *All life and citizen of the world*

Object: *Open letter from the Author*

Dear friends and fellow citizens of the world,

I am reaching out to you as a witness to the persistent shadow that looms over our modern society – a shadow that takes the form of a new, insidious, and utterly unacceptable kind of slavery. Today, I write not only as a communicator but also as someone who feels compelled to shed light on this grave issue. The struggle for freedom continues, and it is a collective responsibility to ensure that the rights and dignity of all are upheld.

My heart, my words, and my pen rise up with determination to fight against this human tragedy that continues to affect millions of innocent souls across the globe. We can no longer remain silent in the face of this fundamental violation of human rights, and that is why I make this appeal to all. In a world where we have made impressive progress, it is inconceivable that modern slavery persists. It takes many forms, from forced labor in dark factories to human trafficking for sexual exploitation. Individuals, often invisible, suffer in appalling conditions.

They deserve our compassion, our solidarity, and above all, our action to put an end to this abomination.

This appeal to all is not simply a request for conscience. It is a cry from the heart, an invitation to stand up and take action. Every person, every voice, every gesture counts in this fight for human dignity. As a writer, I believe in the power of words to illuminate the dark, to inspire thought, and to inspire change.

We can use our pens as weapons to denounce injustice, to raise awareness, and to build a world where every individual is free to live without fear of slavery. We have to start with education. Let's educate ourselves and others about the different forms that modern slavery takes.

It is time to break through the ignorance and face this often-hidden reality. Let's educate our children, families, friends, and communities about the importance of human dignity and the inalienable rights of every human being.

Next, we must support organizations dedicated to the fight against modern slavery. Whether they are working on the ground saving victims, advocating for stronger laws, or providing refuge for survivors.

These organizations are essential in this battle. Let's support them financially, by donating our time, or by sharing their messages to amplify their reach. Finally, we must demand changes at the political and economic level.

We must pressure our governments to take concrete action against modern slavery.

We must encourage companies to ensure that their supply chain is free from all forms of exploitation. Dear friends, together we can make a difference. We can end this terrible reality. Modern slavery cannot coexist with our values of humanity, justice, and freedom. Join me in this call to all so that we can build a world where every human being is free, respected and fulfilled.

Let's make this appeal to all a movement, a force that transcends borders, languages, and cultures. Together, we can eradicate modern slavery and leave a legacy of freedom for future generations. Thank you for joining this vital fight.

With determination,

Kossi!

CONTENT

KO6 Editions

CONCEPT & IDEOLOGY

An idea from the author

The ideology of "modern slavery" is based on a combination of economic, social and political factors that allow the exploitation and domination of individuals under conditions similar to those of historical slavery, although in different forms.

This ideology justifies exploitation by depriving individuals of their fundamental rights, dignity and freedom, often for the benefit of those who take advantage of their forced labor or vulnerable situation. Modern slavery is based on the dehumanization of exploited people, reducing them to objects or mere economic resources. This allows the exploiters to justify their inhumane treatment by denying the intrinsic value of the victims. One of the primary motivations behind modern slavery is financial gain.

The exploiters seek to maximize their profits by using the cheap or free labor power of the exploited, whether it is forced labor in various industries, forced prostitution, human trafficking, etc.

Modern slavery thrives in contexts where economic, social and political inequalities are prevalent. The exploited often come from disadvantaged backgrounds and are denied access to education, health care and other opportunities. The ideology of modern slavery is supported by tactics of psychological manipulation, threats, and violence. The exploiters create conditions of dependency in the victims, preventing them from escaping or seeking help. Modern slavery is often facilitated by corrupt institutions and lax laws. Operators can act with impunity, knowing that victims have little legal recourse and that the authorities could be complicit.

In some cases, it can be seen as a "normal" part of economic or social functioning. The exploiters can rely on public indifference or ignorance to continue their illegal activities. The ideology is based on a profound violation of human rights and human dignity. Fighting this ideology requires concerted efforts from all of us.

The hell box.

Aisha was tired of this life. "Every day it's the same thing," she said. When I looked at his eyes, they were filled with weariness. So I gently put my hand on her shoulder, answering her in a comforting voice, "I know, darling, I know. But you have to keep hope, one day this will all be over, I promise you."

That night, I just wanted to sleep. I had no desire to argue or talk to anyone. We were in a discreet corner of a small dark room. Aisha's face was lit up with a faint glow, she stood next to me like a childhood accomplice. I knew that our situation was very different from that of the carefree friends who once dreamed of a bright future.

Suddenly, a lukewarm water ran over my shoulders. I was so tired that I couldn't get up to close the door. I thought it was rain coming, but the water still ran like a line on my skin and I felt my chest get wet. Startled, I just turned on my side, trying to forget this world in a deep sleep. That's when Aisha 's hand grabbed my shoulders. She was crying hotly. Slowly I tried to wipe away the stealthy tear that had escaped her. "Promise me," she said.

"What?" I whispered to him in a low voice. So she replied, "You will remember me as I once was, won't you?"

I thought I was the only one tired that night, but she seemed even more exhausted than me.

I gently cupped her face in my hands and lifted her gaze to mine. " Aisha , you are and always will be the same amazing person I have known since childhood. Nothing can ever change that." However, our moment of intimacy was broken by the creaking sound of a door. We jumped, and I fell silent instantly. A dark figure appeared in the doorway, followed closely by an icy voice. "No more chatter, no more chatter, girls. The customer is on his way. Get ready to satisfy him," ordered the sinister figure. It was Doria, the manager of the club where we were held captive.

Aisha exchanged a look of anguish with me. I knew his dignity was about to be violated once again. So, she stood beside me, her hands shaking in a silent struggle.

Her VISA expired in 17 days, and it was the only paid job offer that would allow him to stay a few more days in the territory.

"This is slavery," she whispered. "It's just a slavery," I replied. ": It's modern. Modern slavery, for sure. The system is actually designed so that no one forces you, but yourself, you run to the bosses, pining for jobs, the worst ever, whatever the conditions. The rule is to do everything not to be deported." "But what is modern slavery?" Aisha asked me slowly, as if she were still in the 14th century.

Modern slavery, like an elusive specter, extended its sneaky tentacles across the world. The horrors of the practice still raged, despite efforts to end it for decades.

Aisha and I were witnesses to this, confronting this cruel reality that had robbed us of our freedom. Our story just began in this dark corner of the small dark room, imprisoned like common goods.

Aisha's tired looks expressed all the exhaustion of a life subjected to modern slavery. My hand rested gently on her shoulder, trying to bring him some comfort.

"I know, darling, I know. But we must keep hope, one day all this will end, I promise you," I whispered in a comforting voice, well aware of the magnitude of the task ahead. . We were both trapped in this sinister web, facing various forms of exploitation. Modern slavery took on many faces, from debt bondage to human trafficking, including forced labor in various industries. Agriculture, construction, manufacturing, every sector seemed to be plagued by this heinous practice.

Human trafficking, one of the most widespread sinister practices, affected the most vulnerable. People living in poverty, refugees, undocumented people were caught in the cruel nets of ruthless traffickers. Recruited under false promises, they were then subjected to inhuman working conditions for derisory wages. Their rights violated; their vulnerability turned them into easy prey for unscrupulous exploiters. This tragedy spanned the globe, affecting both developing and prosperous nations.

Even the United States, with its strict laws, did not escape the grip of modern slavery. Human trafficking plagued sectors such as agriculture and construction, reminding us that this odious practice ignored borders and regulations. Refugees and migrants who fled conflict and persecution, but found themselves plunged into another form of hell.

Modern slavery took advantage of their economic disarray and precarious status to further exploit them. Human trafficking networks proliferated, turning their dreams of security into an endless nightmare. Amidst this inextricable web of despair, Aisha and I refused to submit. Each of our tears shed was a spark of resistance, each suffering endured strengthened our resolve.

The hope of better days guided my steps. My sufferings and my experience compel me to ask you: Do you know what modern slavery is?

What is it?

Modern slavery refers to the use of forced labour, human trafficking and other forms of exploitation in which individuals are treated as property and forced to work against their will.

This certainly include forms of forced labor such as debt bondage, the credit card system, immigration policies, forced marriage and forced labor in various industries including agriculture, construction, and manufacturing. It is a violation of human rights and a serious problem that affects millions of people around the world.

Modern slavery is a phenomenon that continues to plague the world, despite efforts to end the practice for many years.

I remember Isabella, one of the girls we met that night, and her story. I can remember her words in the exact terms as she was telling us her history. She said:

My life has been a relentless journey through darkness and despair. I was born into a small village in Mexico, a place filled with dreams of a better life beyond the border. Little did I know that my journey would take me from the clutches of one form of slavery to another. My childhood was filled with laughter and dreams, but those were shattered when my family fell into debt. At the tender age of 12, I was forced to leave school and start working in a local factory to help repay the debt. Day by day, my dreams grew distant, replaced by the harsh reality of long hours, exhaustion, and mistreatment. I was trapped, a modern-day slave in my own country.

When I turned 18, my family's desperation led us to believe that crossing into the United States would offer salvation. We were told tales of opportunity and freedom, but what awaited us was far from it. The journey across the border was treacherous, and we were at the mercy of ruthless coyotes.

The moment we set foot in the US; we were seized by traffickers who saw us as nothing more than commodities to be exploited. It was a chilly evening in November when the nightmare truly began. My heart raced as a group of men surrounded us, their faces hidden in the shadows. Their harsh whispers and calloused hands tore us away from our families, and we were thrust into a van, our pleas falling on deaf ears.

The van journeyed through the night, the rattling wheels echoing our fear and uncertainty. We arrived at a dimly lit warehouse, its cold concrete floors a stark contrast to the warmth we had once known. The traffickers laughed among themselves as they gave us new names – mine was now Maria. They stripped us of our identities, leaving us vulnerable and voiceless. The nights turned into an endless cycle of flashing lights and booming music as we were paraded like commodities for the highest bidder. In the early hours of the morning, we were herded like cattle into the back of a dingy nightclub.

The stench of alcohol and desperation hung heavy in the air. As the music throbbed and the neon lights flickered, we were forced to dance, our bodies moving in ways we never thought possible.

Men leered and groped, their lustful gazes making our skin crawl. Days blended into nights, and time lost its meaning as we were shuffled from one location to another. Sometimes, we found ourselves in luxurious penthouses, catering to the whims of powerful men. Other times, we were in seedy motels, the harshness of our reality magnified by the flickering fluorescent lights. As the years wore on, we became shadows of our former selves. The initial spark of defiance dimmed as we succumbed to the rhythm of survival. The only solace was the bond we formed – the women who became my sisters, my confidantes, my lifeline. We whispered stories of hope and escape in hushed tones, our dreams serving as a flickering light in the darkness.

After 23 grueling years, a glimmer of hope emerged. An undercover agent infiltrated our captors' network, offering us a chance at freedom. It was a moonless night in July when chaos erupted. We seized the moment, running through back alleys, our hearts pounding with equal parts fear and determination. Sirens wailed in the distance as we sprinted towards the flashing lights of border patrol vehicles. Standing on American soil, tears mixed with relief streamed down our faces. We had broken free from the chains that had bound us for so long. The road to recovery was arduous, but we were no longer imprisoned by our captors' cruelty. In shelters, we began to piece our lives back together, healing each other's wounds with newfound strength and resilience. She stood like a survivor.

Her journey from a village in Mexico to the depths of darkness in the United States is a story of endurance, of emerging from the depths of despair into the light of hope.

"Through the horrors of trafficking and exploitation, I clung to my identity and my dreams, proving that the human spirit can triumph over even the darkest of circumstances" she said. The days following her escape were a blur of emotions – relief, disbelief, and a newfound sense of freedom that we were only beginning to comprehend. The shelter we found ourselves in was a haven, a place where our stories were met with empathy rather than skepticism. As the days turned into weeks, we underwent counseling and therapy to heal the scars that weren't visible on our bodies.

The wounds ran deep, the memories of abuse and exploitation haunting our dreams.

But together, we navigated the path to recovery. The bond we shared, forged in the crucible of suffering, was a lifeline that pulled us out of the abyss. With the assistance of social workers and legal experts, we began to piece together the shattered fragments of our identities. We embraced our real names once again, shedding the aliases that had been forced upon us.

The process of reclaiming our true selves was both liberating and painful, a reminder of the resilience that had carried us through the darkest of times. As the years went by, we found strength not only in each other but also in our shared determination to prevent others from falling into the same trap. I remember the day I stood before a crowd, sharing my story for the first time.

The room was hushed as I spoke of the horrors I had endured, but my voice remained steady. In the eyes of those listening, I saw empathy, compassion, and a desire for change. My story was no longer just mine – it was a testament to the resilience of the human spirit and a call to action against the darkness that still persisted in the shadows. As I look back on my friend's journey from a small village in Mexico to the stages of nightclubs in the United States, I am reminded of the indomitable spirit that resides within us all. While the road to healing is long and fraught with challenges, it is a journey worth undertaking.

For in the midst of adversity, we discover the strength to break free from the chains that bind us and emerge as survivors, ready to rewrite the narrative of our lives. The path to healing and empowerment was not without its hurdles.

As the years passed, the traffickers who had once held us captive began to face justice. Law enforcement agencies, armed with the information we had provided, dismantled networks and arrested key perpetrators. It was a cathartic moment, knowing that our testimonies had played a role in bringing about justice and closure for countless individuals who had suffered. One particularly poignant chapter in our journey was the annual "Survivors' Day," a commemoration of our strength, resilience, and unity. It was a day to honor those who hadn't made it out and a day to acknowledge the battles that continued beyond escape. Survivors from around the world gathered to share stories of triumph and to remind one another that they were never alone.

Every scar, every trial, and every victory shaped me into the person I am today – a survivor, a mentor, an advocate. And as I stand here. "You're still young, go to

school or find a church to help you out. Leave this life",
said Isabella. I am acutely aware that my journey is just one
thread in the tapestry of countless survivors who refuse to
be defined by their past.

Isabella was a good friend for Us at the beginning,
but not for long.

Modern slavery is different from historical slavery,
which was legally recognized and institutionalized.
Human trafficking is one of the most common forms of
modern slavery. Victims of trafficking are often recruited
under false promises of employment or education, then
transported across borders and forced to work in
inhumane conditions.

Those most vulnerable to trafficking are people
living in poverty, refugees, and undocumented people.

African and south America countries are particularly affected, but there are also cases of modern slavery in developed countries.

The United States, for example, has strict laws against human trafficking, but there are still cases of modern slavery in industries such as agriculture and construction.

In terms of immigration and refugees, the phenomenon of modern slavery tends to worsen in situations of humanitarian crises and armed conflicts. People who flee their country because of violence or persecution are often more vulnerable to exploitation, as they find themselves in situations of economic distress and are often undocumented.

Refugees and migrants are also often victims of human trafficking, which can lead to them being exploited

in industries such as agriculture, construction, and manufacturing.

There has also been an increase in the number of refugees and migrants crossing borders illegally, making them even more vulnerable to human trafficking networks.

Trafficking networks take advantage of the situation of refugees and migrants to recruit and exploit them, often by forcing them to work in inhuman conditions or by prostituting them. Restrictive migration policies contribute to the rise of modern slavery. People who are blocked at the border or who are turned back to their country of origin are often more vulnerable to exploitation.

REAL CASES

Case KF094331_00H: United States

During his tenure, the administration of the former President of the United States adopted policies that contributed to the phenomenon of modern slavery. Some of these policies included: Restricted immigration policies that have made it harder for people to escape modern slavery situations in their home countries and seek refuge in the United States.

Detention policies for asylum seekers that have led to inhumane detention conditions and made it more difficult for asylum seekers to claim their rights. Policies that have fostered the exploitation of temporary foreign workers, including reducing protections for workers and making it harder for workers to report abuse.

Policies that have limited the ability of human rights organizations and non-governmental organizations to monitor and report human rights abuses.

Importantly, these policies have been widely criticized by human rights organizations and non-governmental organizations, as well as other civil society actors. The new policies adopted by the new US administration could improve the situation, but it will take time to assess their effectiveness.

It should be remembered that "family separation" policies had been put in place which led to tens of thousands of family separations for reasons related to immigration.

These policies have fostered the exploitation of temporary foreign workers, expanding the modern slavery industry, including reducing protections for workers and making it harder for workers to report abuse.

Remember also that the President wanted to limit H1-B visas, which allow American companies to hire only highly qualified foreign workers.

These policies have also limited the ability of human rights organizations and non-governmental organizations to monitor and report human rights abuses.

Recently a new that no one wanted to read again is Romario's childhood.

Romario's story is a tragic testament to the repercussions of policies that allowed modern slavery to thrive. At the tender age of 11, Romario found himself torn apart from his mother due to the "family separation" policies put in place during the former administration in the United States. The date was etched into his memory – a day that marked the beginning of a harrowing journey into the depths of exploitation.

Separated from his family and stripped of his innocence, Romario was thrust into an unfamiliar world. His mother's desperate pleas echoed in his mind as he was taken away to a farm on the outskirts of New York City. The date of his arrival there was the start of a grim chapter in his life. The farm, a place that should have been filled with the joy of nature, became a prison of forced labor. Romario's days were long and grueling, characterized by backbreaking work from dawn till dusk. The conditions were deplorable, with little regard for his well-being or safety. He toiled under the sweltering sun, enduring physical and emotional abuse that no child should ever experience.

As the seasons changed, Romario's resilience grew. He found solace in the small moments, the fleeting memories

of his family, and dreams of reuniting with them someday. Yet, as time passed, hope began to fade, replaced by the bleak reality of his circumstances.

But just as darkness seemed to engulf Romario's world, a glimmer of light emerged. It was a day like any other, yet different – a day that would alter his fate forever. An organization dedicated to combating modern slavery and supporting survivors launched a rescue operation in the area. Guided by their determination and unwavering belief in justice, they infiltrated the farm.

The date of his rescue is etched into Romario's heart as a symbol of a second chance at life. The rescue team's arrival was a testament to the power of compassion and solidarity. They liberated Romario and his fellow captives, freeing them from the chains of exploitation that had bound them for so long. Upon his rescue, Romario was not

just given his freedom back, but also a chance to reclaim his stolen childhood. He was provided with access to education, counseling, and a supportive environment that fostered his healing. Over time, Romario's spirit rekindled, and his dreams of reuniting with his family gained new strength.

The story of Romario serves as a poignant reminder of the deep-seated consequences of policies that prioritize profit over humanity. While his journey was marked by adversity, his resilience, and the compassion of those who rescued him stand as a beacon of hope in the fight against modern slavery. The date of his rescue represents a turning point – a day when Romario's story shifted from one of suffering to one of survival and the indomitable human spirit.

Case 0018234: Rapid Subway

The 2014 case of the Subway fast food chain in the United States: Investigators found employees working in modern slavery conditions in New York and Indiana. Employees were forced to work unpaid overtime, sleep in unacceptable conditions and receive very low wages. In 2014, an investigation by US authorities uncovered a modern slavery scandal at Subway restaurants in the United States. Investigators found employees of Mexican descent working in modern-slavery conditions at Subway restaurants in New York and Indiana.

Employees were forced to work unpaid overtime, sleep in unacceptable conditions, and receive very low wages. According to employee testimonies, they were forced to work up to 80 hours a week without being paid for overtime.

They were also forced to sleep in unsanitary rooms with several other employees, without access to proper sanitary facilities.

Employers were also accused of withholding employees' wages and threatening to send them back to Mexico if they complained. This scandal led to lawsuits against employers and legal actions to recover unpaid wages.

It also led to policy changes at Subway to ensure employees are treated fairly and to avoid such situations in the future. This case shows the importance of monitoring and regulation to protect migrant workers from modern exploitation.

It is also important to raise awareness among employers and consumers of the risks of modern migrant

exploitation and to put in place policies to protect the

rights of migrant workers.

Case of Florida Tomatoes: 2010

Investigators found migrant workers from Central and South America working in modern slavery conditions on a tomato farm in Florida. Employees were forced to work unpaid overtime, sleep in unacceptable conditions and receive very low wages. Employees were forced to work unpaid overtime, sleep in unacceptable conditions and receive very low wages. According to the testimonies of the employees, they were forced to work up to 12 hours a day, 7 days a week without being paid for overtime.

Employers have also been accused of holding them against their will in unsanitary barracks and threatening to send them back to their country of origin if they complain.

Employers have also been accused of denying them medical care and failing to uphold workplace safety standards.

This scandal led to lawsuits against employers and legal actions to recover unpaid wages. It has also led to policy changes to ensure that employers comply with workers' rights laws and to avoid such situations in the future. This case shows the importance of monitoring and regulation to protect migrant workers from modern exploitation.

In the heart of the Sunshine State, beneath the sprawling expanse of Florida's tomato farms, a story of suffering and strength unfolded. Maria's tale, like so many others, was woven into the very fabric of those fields – a testament to the shadows that can stretch even under the brightest sun. With a heart heavy with hope, Maria had journeyed from her village in Central America, seeking a future brighter than the past she left behind. The allure of distant dreams beckoned her, promising prosperity and a chance to secure her family's future.

But what awaited her on that Florida farm was a harsh reality far removed from the promises that had lured her across borders.

Days blurred into nights as Maria and her fellow workers toiled relentlessly, a never-ending cycle dictated by the sun's rise and fall. The rhythm of their lives was set not by choice but by the harsh commands of those who held power over their fates. Their hands, once gentle, were now calloused and scarred from unyielding labor. In the beginning, the assurances of fair pay were whispered like a distant melody, but the notes never quite reached their ears. Instead, their wages remained meager, a cruel joke that stung with every pittance received. The promise of overtime pay was yet another illusion, a mirage shimmering in the distance but forever out of reach. Long after the sun dipped below the horizon, they toiled on, unpaid and unseen.

Their quarters, if they could be called that, were nothing more than wretched hovels – cramped spaces that echoed with the silent cries of the oppressed. As the moon painted the world in shades of darkness, Maria clung to broken slumber, haunted by the uncertainty of tomorrow.

But fear was a constant companion, one that gnawed at their souls. Threats of deportation hung over them like storm clouds, suffocating their dreams and stifling their voices. To speak out was to invite retribution, a truth etched into their hearts like a scar.

Injuries became part of their daily existence, but medical care was a luxury denied. The employers turned a blind eye, their eyes fixed on profit margins rather than the well-being of those who made those profits possible. Safety was an afterthought, a fleeting notion that dissolved in the face of unrelenting demand.

Yet, amid the darkness, a glimmer of hope arose. Investigators arrived on the scene, drawn by whispers of injustice that had finally reached the world beyond those fields. Their presence was a lifeline, a promise of salvation in a world that had turned a blind eye for too long.

The date of their arrival became a beacon of change. Lawsuits were filed, and the battle for justice commenced. With trembling voices, workers like Maria shared their stories, each word a testament to the resilience of the human spirit. The fight was arduous, the path riddled with obstacles, but with every step, they drew closer to the light. In the aftermath, as legal battles raged on, policy changes emerged from the ashes.

The date of those changes marked a new chapter, one where the rights of workers were recognized, and the shackles of exploitation began to crack. Maria's journey, from that Florida farm to the halls of justice, was a testament to the power of resilience, to the unyielding strength that courses through those who dare to stand against injustice.

The scars from those days would forever linger, etched into the tapestry of her being. Yet, as the date of her liberation stood tall, Maria emerged not as a victim but as a survivor – a living embodiment of the unwavering spirit that refuses to be broken by the chains of modern slavery.

Case 095864: Textiles in Burma

Investigators discovered that migrant workers from Burma were working in modern slavery conditions in the textile industry, they were forced to work unpaid overtime, sleep in unacceptable conditions and receive very low wages, they were also subjected to physical and psychological violence.

In 2016, an investigation by British authorities uncovered a modern slavery scandal at a cleaning company in Britain. Investigators discovered that migrant workers from Eastern Europe were working in conditions of modern slavery at this company.

Employees were forced to work unpaid overtime, sleep in unacceptable conditions and receive very low wages.

According to employee testimonies, they were forced to work up to 80 hours a week without being paid for overtime.

They were also forced to sleep in unsanitary rooms with several other employees, without access to proper sanitary facilities. Employers have also been accused of withholding employees' wages and threatening to send them back to their home countries if they complain. This scandal led to lawsuits against employers and legal actions to recover unpaid wages.

Case 2022649670: Qatar

The case of migrant workers on construction sites in Qatar for the olympics in 2022. Migrant workers, mainly from South Asia, have been victims of modern slavery on construction sites for the 2022 olympics in Qatar.

Employees were forced to work unpaid overtime, sleep in unacceptable conditions and receive very low wages, they were also subjected to physical and psychological abuse. These examples show that modern slavery is a global phenomenon affecting migrant workers in various economic sectors and in various countries.

Case 8756645 Australia

In 2020, an investigation by Australian authorities uncovered a modern slavery scandal at a construction company in Australia. Investigators discovered that migrant workers from Asia were working in conditions of modern slavery at this company. Employees were forced to work unpaid overtime, sleep in unacceptable conditions, and receive very low wages.

According to the testimonies of the employees, they were forced to work up to 15 hours a day, 7 days a week without being paid for overtime. Employers have also been accused of holding them against their will in unsanitary barracks.

Employers have also been accused of denying them medical care and failing to meet workplace safety standards . This scandal led to lawsuits against employers and legal actions to recover unpaid wages.

It has also led to policy changes to ensure that employers comply with workers' rights laws and to avoid such situations in the future.

This case shows the importance of monitoring and regulation to protect migrant workers from modern exploitation. Testimony of Raj, a Worker at the Australian Construction Company (2020)

Amid the vibrant tapestry of Australia's modern landscape, a tale of despair and resilience emerged in the year 2020: Raj's testimony.

Raj, a migrant worker seeking a new life, unwittingly stepped into the heart of a construction company, where shadows of modern slavery lurked beneath the glistening façade. What was meant to be a path towards prosperity turned into a journey through darkness, a labyrinth of exploitation that defied the promise of a better future.

The first rays of the sun had barely kissed the horizon when Raj and his fellow workers were thrust into a relentless cycle of labor. Days stretched into nights, their bodies echoing the rhythm of unending toil. The company's hollow assurance of fair compensation proved nothing more than a fleeting mirage.

Instead, their wages trickled in as mere droplets, barely enough to appease hunger's relentless call. Overtime, a twisted mockery of justice, saw them laboring for hours beyond measure, yet their pockets remained empty.

As daylight faded, Raj's tired footsteps would lead him to barracks that masqueraded as shelter. The promise of rest was a cruel joke, as the squalid conditions shackled him to discomfort. Sleep was elusive, and his dreams were drowned by the weight of the endless cycle that had ensnared him.

Fear crept into every corner of his existence. Threats of deportation dangled over him like a sword, stifling his voice and condemning him to silence.

The employers held his fate within their grasp, and dissent was met with consequences too dire to fathom.

The plight of Raj and his fellow workers extended far beyond labor – their health was an afterthought, their injuries disregarded. Workplace safety was a distant dream, casualties of an unfeeling system that valued profit over their well-being.

Yet, in the midst of this darkness, a glimmer of hope pierced through. Investigators arrived like beacons of justice, their presence a promise of redemption. As Raj recounted his story, the shackles of silence began to crumble. The date of their intervention became a turning point, the moment when their cries were finally heard.

The pursuit of justice led to lawsuits, a testament to the collective strength of those who had suffered in silence.

The battle for their rights was fierce, marked by determination and unwavering resolve. With each step, a new dawn emerged, casting aside the shadows that had once held them captive.

Case 245234:Italy

Organizations denounce modern slavery in Italy and fight against this form of inhuman treatment.

These organizations include Caritas, the National Committee for Human Rights, the Italian Committee for UNICEF, Amnesty International, and the Italian Platform against Modern Slavery. It is important to note that modern slavery is a complex problem that requires a comprehensive approach to be effectively combated.

The Italian authorities have taken steps to combat this problem, but much more needs to be done to end the exploitation of migrants in Italy.

Modern slavery in Italy operates primarily by exploiting migrants seeking to enter the country to find employment and a better future. Migrants may be promised work and housing, but once they arrive in Italy they often find themselves in situations of exploitation and inhuman treatment. Migrants may be forced to work in unsafe and underpaid conditions, often without having signed a contract of employment or having access to social or legal protections.

Employers can also withhold identity papers or identity documents from migrants, preventing them from quitting their jobs or reporting abuse.

There are also cases of modern slavery in the area of prostitution, where migrants are forced into prostitution against their will and are subjected to physical and psychological violence and abuse.

It is important to note that criminal networks are often involved in these exploitative activities, using threat, violence and manipulation to keep victims in a state of submission. Italian authorities have taken steps to combat these forms of modern slavery, but much more needs to be done to end these inhumane practices.

Case A00938: Libya

Modern slavery in Libya. exploitation of migrants, examples, places, dates, and reporting organizations .

In Libya, modern slavery is a serious problem that primarily affects migrants seeking to cross the country to Europe. Since the fall of the Gaddafi regime in 2011, Libya has become a transit point for migrants from sub-Saharan Africa and other regions, seeking to escape poverty and conflict in their country of origin. Many migrants in Libya are exposed to forms of exploitation and inhuman treatment, such as forced labour, kidnapping, torture and sexual violence. Migrants may be held in illegal detention centers where they are subjected to inhumane conditions and exploited for their labor or for resale.

Criminal networks are often implicated in these exploitative activities, using threats, violence and manipulation to keep victims in a state of submission.

Prostitution

There are also cases of modern slavery in the area of prostitution, where migrants are forced into prostitution against their will and are subjected to physical and psychological violence and abuse.

Many organizations denounce modern slavery in Libya, such as Amnesty International, Human Rights Watch, and the International Organization for Migration (IOM), which have documented cases of abuse and called on the Libyan authorities to take action. to protect migrants from exploitation and abuse.

However, due to the unstable situation in Libya, it is difficult for these organizations to act effectively on the ground. There have been numerous reports documenting cases of modern slavery in Libya in recent years:

In November 2017, CNN released footage showing men being auctioned off as slaves in Libya.

The images sparked an international reaction of condemnation and led the Libyan authorities to open an investigation.

In December 2017, the International Organization for Migration (IOM) reported that thousands of migrants in Libya were subjected to forms of exploitation and inhuman treatment, including forced labour, kidnapping, torture and beatings. sexual.

In January 2018, Amnesty International published a report entitled " Libya's Dark Web of Collusion", in which he denounced the abuses committed against migrants in Libya, including modern slavery, and called on the Libyan authorities to take measures to protect migrants against exploitation and mistreatment.

In April 2018, Human Rights Watch also published a report entitled " Libya's Migrant Detention Crisis: Summary Execution , Torture, Rape , and Forced Labour".

In this report, the organization denounces the abuses committed against migrants in Libya and calls on the Libyan authorities to take measures to protect migrants against exploitation and mistreatment.

In September 2018, the European Commission launched a program to rescue migrants in distress in Libya and to reduce migration flows to Europe.

However, several NGOs have denounced the inhuman conditions in Libyan detention centers where migrants were held and highlighted the risk of modern slavery.

Case: Roxham road in Canada

The Roxham Road, which connects Canada to the United States, has become a frequent crossing point for asylum seekers seeking to enter Canada. Some have accused Canadian authorities of using this route to lure asylum seekers and exploit them once they enter Canada.

There is no concrete evidence that Canadian authorities are deliberately using the Roxham Road to lure asylum seekers and exploit them.

However, it is true that asylum seekers passing through this route are subject to difficult conditions, including delays in asylum processes, prolonged detentions and precarious living conditions.

In 2018, reports emerged that asylum seekers who crossed Roxham Road were placed in overcrowded and under-staffed detention centers or temporary reception centres. Asylum seekers also faced delays in asylum processes, which left them in limbo for long periods of time.

In 2020, reports emerged that asylum seekers who crossed the Roxham Road faced difficulties accessing healthcare, education and other essential public services. Asylum seekers have also faced discrimination and violence based on their migration status. It is important to note that these examples are not exhaustive and there are many other cases where asylum seekers who have crossed the Roxham Road have faced difficulties.

International organizations, NGOs and civil society actors continue to monitor conditions for asylum seekers crossing Roxham Road and to report human rights abuses.

Several organisations, NGOs and civil society actors have denounced the conditions for asylum seekers crossing the Roxham road:

Amnesty International published a report in 2018 which denounced the inhumane detention conditions for asylum seekers crossing Roxham Road.

Quebec's Commission des droits de la personne et des droits de la jeunesse issued an opinion in 2018 that denounced the inhumane detention conditions for asylum seekers crossing Roxham Road.

The United Nations Refugee Organization (UNHCR) issued a statement in 2018 decrying delays in asylum processes for asylum seekers crossing Roxham Road.

The Canadian Civil Liberties Association (CCLA)
filed a complaint in 2019 that denounced the inhumane
detention conditions for asylum seekers crossing Roxham
Road.

Note: Amnesty International published another report in 2020 which exposed the
difficulties for asylum seekers crossing the Roxham road to access healthcare, education
and other essential public services.

Case: Dark Web of Collusion

In January 2018, Amnesty International published a report entitled " Libya's Dark Web of Collusion", in which he denounced the abuses committed against migrants in Libya. According to this report, thousands of migrants, mainly from sub-Saharan Africa and other regions, are exposed to forms of exploitation and of inhuman treatment, including forced labour, confinement, torture and sexual violence.

The report describes how migrants are often held in illegal detention centers or labor camps, where they are subjected to inhumane conditions and where they are exploited for their labor or for resale.

Criminal networks are often implicated in these exploitative activities, using threats, violence and manipulation to keep victims in a state of submission.

The report also denounces the Libyan authorities for their lack of will to protect migrants against exploitation and ill-treatment, and for their collusion with criminal networks that take advantage of the situation of migrants. Amnesty International is calling on the Libyan authorities to take action to protect migrants from exploitation and abuse, and to prosecute those who abuse migrants. It is important to underline that this Amnesty International report is one of many documenting abuses against migrants in Libya.

Since 2011, Libya has become a transit point for migrants from sub-Saharan Africa and other regions seeking to escape poverty and conflict in their country of origin. However, the volatile security and political situation in Libya has made it difficult for the Libyan authorities and humanitarian organizations to act effectively to protect migrants from exploitation and abuse.

brazil

There are cases of modern slavery in Brazil, mainly involving migrant workers who are exploited in various sectors such as agriculture, construction, mining, and production factories.

The places where this happens are usually in rural areas and industrial areas of the country, such as Pará, Mato Grosso, Goiás, and Minas Gerais.

There have been cases of exploitation of migrant workers in agriculture, where they are subjected to extremely harsh working conditions, underpaid and without access to social or legal protections. There are also cases of exploitation in mines, where workers are subjected to dangerous working conditions and are paid very little. There are organizations that denounce modern slavery in Brazil and fight against this form of inhuman treatment. These organizations include the Ministry of Labour, the Ministry of Justice, the Pastoral Land Commission (CPT), and the Movement of Landless Rural Workers (MST).

These organizations are involved in the implementation of prevention and reintegration programs for migrant workers who are victims of modern slavery.

"

Modern slavery is a complex problem that requires a comprehensive approach to be effectively combated. Brazilian authorities have taken steps to combat this problem, but much more needs to be done to end the exploitation of migrants in Brazil

Panama _

There are cases of modern slavery in Panama, mainly involving migrant workers who are exploited in various sectors such as agriculture, construction, mining and production factories. The places where this happens are usually in rural areas and industrial areas of the country, such as the region of Chiriqui, Coclé, Herrera, and West Panama. There have been cases of exploitation of migrant workers in agriculture, where they are subjected to extremely harsh working conditions, underpaid.

There are also cases of exploitation in mines, where workers are subjected to dangerous working conditions and are paid very little.

There are organizations that denounce modern slavery in Panama and fight against this form of inhuman treatment.

These organizations include the Ministry of Labor and Employment, the Ministry of Justice, the International Organization for Migration (IOM), and the Department for Social Affairs of the Presidency of the Republic.

These organizations are involved in the implementation of prevention and reintegration programs for migrant workers who are victims of modern slavery. It is important to note that modern slavery is a complex problem that requires a comprehensive approach to be effectively combated. Panamanian authorities have taken steps to combat this problem, but much more needs to be done to end the exploitation of migrants in Panama. In January 2019, the Ministry of Labor and Employment announced that it had freed 22 migrant workers who were held in modern slavery on a sugar cane farm in the Chiriqui region.

In June 2019, the Ministry of Labor announced that it had freed 12 migrant workers who were being held in modern slavery at an illegal gold mine in the Coclé region.

In July 2019, the Ministry of Labor announced that it had freed 16 migrant workers who were held in modern slavery at a timber production factory in the Panama West region.

It is unclear whether there have been any deaths related to modern slavery in Panama, but it is likely that migrant workers who fall victim to these forms of exploitation experience extremely harsh working conditions and risk serious physical and mental harm.

It is important to note that cases of modern slavery may be under-reported and there may be unreported cases of deaths linked to this form of exploitation.

Panamanian authorities and humanitarian organizations continue to work to combat modern slavery and protect migrant workers from abuse and mistreatment.

The immigration routes.

The illegal immigration route through the forests of Panama can contribute to the phenomenon of mistreatment and modern slavery. Migrants seeking to enter the United States or Canada illegally often cross into Panama using illegal routes through the forests. These routes are often dangerous and migrants may be exposed to risks such as violence, abuse, disease and accidents. Migrants using these illegal routes are often vulnerable to criminal networks that take advantage of their situation.

Migrants may be forced to work in inhuman conditions, underpaid, without access to social or legal protections.

These criminal networks may also use threats, violence and manipulation to keep victims in a state of submission.

The situation is further complicated by the fact that these illegal migrants are often considered criminals by Panamanian authorities, making it difficult for them to report abuse and receive legal or medical help. Humanitarian organizations and Panamanian authorities are working together to protect migrants from abuse and mistreatment, but much more needs to be done to end this form of exploitation.

THE CAUSES

Governments

Some governments promote the exploitation of migrants, and we must fight, work, and denounce these practices. These governments have several methods of acting, among others:

Restrictive migration policies: Policies that limit legal recourse for migrants can prevent them from seeking help and reporting cases of modern slavery. Policies that limit access to employment and social services can also make them more vulnerable to exploiters.

Detention and Detention of Migrants: Governments that detain and detain migrants can make them vulnerable to physical and psychological abuse, and they can be forced to work in inhumane conditions.

Weak Penalties for Slave Employers: Governments that fail to take effective steps to prosecute and punish slave employers can further the exploitation of migrants by giving employers impunity for their illegal behavior.

Weak protection of workers' rights: Governments that do not have an effective system to protect workers' rights can foster the exploitation of migrants by offering them little recourse to report and combat abuses.

Weak international cooperation: Governments that do not cooperate effectively with other countries to combat human trafficking and modern slavery can foster modern slavery.

The refusal of some governments to give residence papers to migrants can contribute to modern exploitation.

Migrants who do not have valid residency papers are often considered illegal and may be excluded from legal systems of protection and redress. They are often seen as people without status and are therefore more vulnerable to exploitation.

Migrants without valid residency papers are often forced to work in dangerous and inhumane conditions, as they have few legal avenues to report abuses and seek redress. Employers can also exploit them by not paying them the minimum wage or failing to meet health and safety standards.

The so-called "without papers". Migrants without valid residency papers are also more vulnerable to human trafficking and modern slavery, as they are often recruited under false promises and transported across borders to be exploited in inhumane conditions.

Employment discrimination: Migrants may face employment discrimination because of their migration status, ethnicity, race, religion, gender or sexual orientation . This can prevent them from finding legal employment and force them to accept precarious and poorly paid jobs, or to work in dangerous and inhumane conditions.

Discrimination in access to services: Migrants may face discrimination in access to basic services such as health, education, housing and social care.

This can prevent them from benefiting from the services necessary to maintain a decent quality of life and make them more vulnerable to exploitation.

The criminalization of migrants: The policies and practices that criminalize migrants.

Deportation: Immigrants to their country of origin can promote modern exploitation.

Deportation can make immigrants more vulnerable to exploitation, as they may find themselves in a precarious economic situation and undocumented in their country of origin.

Deported immigrants may have difficulty finding legal employment and accessing basic social services, as they may be stigmatized and discriminated against due to their deported status. This may force them to accept precarious and poorly paid jobs, or to work in dangerous and inhumane conditions.

Deported immigrants may also be more vulnerable to human trafficking and modern slavery, as they may be recruited under false promises and transported across borders to be exploited in inhumane conditions .

Human trafficking networks can also take advantage of their situation to recruit and exploit them.

Deportation policies also cause painful family separations and can have psychological and emotional consequences for deported immigrants and their families. The deportation of immigrants to their countries of origin can foster modern exploitation by making immigrants more vulnerable to economic exploitation, exposing them to the risks of human trafficking and preventing them from accessing legal systems of protection and redress.

Imposition of taxes. Imposing taxes on new immigrants can contribute to modern exploitation by increasing costs for immigrants and making it more difficult for them to settle and integrate into their new country.

Taxes imposed on new immigrants may include registration fees, visa application fees, visa renewal fees, naturalization fees, and taxes on services such as education and health. These taxes can be high and difficult to pay for immigrants who have few financial resources, which may force them to accept precarious and poorly paid jobs, or to work in dangerous and inhumane conditions to raise the necessary money.

In addition, the imposition of taxes may also deter some immigrants from applying for residence papers or work permits, which may make them more vulnerable to exploitation, as they are considered illegal and may be excluded from legal systems. protection and remedy.

The so-called "voluntary" immigration.

Can we say that immigrants and asylum seekers who voluntarily leave their country to live in another country are also the cause of these phenomena? *Of course not !* Immigrants and asylum seekers who voluntarily leave their country to live in another country are not the cause of modern exploitation. People who migrate voluntarily often do so for economic reasons, to improve their quality of life, to escape poverty, violence or persecution.

However, it is important to note that immigrants and asylum seekers can become vulnerable to modern exploitation due to restrictive migration policies, employment discrimination, discrimination in access to services, the criminalization of migrants and deportation.

These factors can make immigrants and asylum seekers more vulnerable to economic exploitation and human trafficking.

We must continue to raise awareness of these issues and work to protect the rights of immigrants and asylum seekers, whether they are there voluntarily or not.

Fictitious Laws

Laws against modern slavery are often fictitious and ineffective for certain reasons:

Difficulty identifying victims : Victims of modern slavery can be difficult to identify because they may be exploited in isolated locations or in situations where they are afraid to report their exploitation.

Victims can also be people who have been trafficked across borders, making their identification even more difficult.

The complexity of the supply chain : Modern slavery can occur at different levels of the supply chain, which makes it difficult to identify responsibilities and put in place effective sanctions.

Weak international cooperation : Human trafficking is a transnational phenomenon that requires international cooperation to be effectively combated.

However, cooperation may be limited due to cultural, legal and political differences between countries.

Weak capacity of judicial and administrative authorities : Judicial and administrative authorities may lack the means, skills or will to effectively implement laws against modern slavery. Authorities can also be corrupt and favor employers and traffickers.

Low employer and consumer awareness: Employers and consumers may be unaware of the risks of modern slavery in their supply chains and in the products they purchase.

It is therefore important to make employers and consumers aware of the risks of modern slavery so that they can take measures to avoid the exploitation of workers.

Low allocation of resources for the fight against modern slavery : Governments may not allocate enough resources for the fight against modern slavery, which makes it difficult to put in place effective actions.

Low involvement of victims: Victims of modern slavery may not be involved in processes to combat modern slavery, which makes it difficult to understand the needs of victims and put in place effective actions.

The policy

It is true that some governments may pass laws against modern slavery for purely political reasons, without actually implementing or enforcing them. This can happen for different reasons, including:

Just to conform to international standards: Governments may pass anti-modern slavery laws to conform to international standards, but not actually implement them.

To look good: Governments may pass anti-modern slavery laws to look good to international organizations or trading partners, but not actually implement them.

To distract: Governments may pass anti-modern slavery laws to distract from larger issues or to mask policies that promote worker exploitation.

The case of asylum seekers

In the case of asylum seekers, the phenomenon of modern slavery is often linked to their situation of vulnerability and their uncertain legal status.

Asylum seekers are often people fleeing situations of violence and persecution in their country of origin, and they can find themselves in situations of uncertainty and precariousness when they arrive in a new country. Asylum seekers can be exploited in temporary reception and detention situations, where they are often placed in detention centers or closed reception centres.

These situations can make them vulnerable to physical and psychological abuse, and they can be forced to work in inhumane conditions.

Asylum seekers are also victims of exploitation in their host country. They often face obstacles in finding legal employment.

They also face barriers in accessing basic social services. Asylum seekers may be forced to work in dangerous and inhumane conditions for extremely low wages, construction and manufacturing. Restrictive asylum policies may also contribute to the rise of modern slavery among asylum seekers. These policies that limit legal recourse for asylum seekers can prevent them from seeking help and reporting cases of modern slavery.

The 1954 convention

The 1954 Convention for the Suppression of Trafficking in Persons and Slavery is an international treaty adopted by the United Nations in 1954. It aims to combat human trafficking and *modern slavery* by criminalizing these practices and encouraging states to cooperate to eradicate them.

The convention defines human trafficking as "any form of acquisition or transfer of persons, by recruitment, transportation, transfer, harboring or receipt, or by any other means, for their exploitation", and modern slavery as " any form of slavery or practices similar to slavery, such as bondage, debt slavery and all forms of exploitation of the prostitution of others". States parties are required to take measures to criminalize these practices and to prosecute and punish the perpetrators of these crimes.

They are also required to cooperate to exchange information and to assist victims of human trafficking and modern slavery.

The 1954 Convention has been ratified by over 120 countries and continues to be an important tool in the fight against human trafficking and modern slavery.

However, it is important to note that *the implementation of the Convention remains a challenge* for many countries, due to the complexity of the criminal networks involved in these activities and the gaps in the legal and judicial systems.

Evil in the Convention. Some of the provisions of the 1954 Convention for the Suppression of Trafficking in Persons and Modern Slavery may contribute to the modern exploitation of migrants in the following cases:

The definition of trafficking in human beings contained in the Convention focuses on the recruitment, transportation and reception of people for their exploitation, but does not *cover* situations where people migrate voluntarily but are then exploited by their employer. This can make it difficult to prosecute employers who exploit voluntary migrant workers.

The Convention focuses on the suppression of trafficking and modern slavery, *but does not deal* underlying causes of forced migration, such as poverty, violence and persecution. It is important to address the underlying causes to reduce the risks of modern exploitation.

Parts of the agreement *are not sufficiently enforced* or have insufficient monitoring mechanisms, making it difficult to ensure that employers respect health and safety standards, minimum wages and workers' rights. The Convention *does not sufficiently address* issues related to restrictive migration policies, which can make migrants vulnerable.

There are other points in the 1954 Convention for the Suppression of Trafficking in Persons and Modern Slavery that may contribute to the modern exploitation of migrants: The Convention does not sufficiently address issues related to *the exploitation migrants* , which can include low wages, unsafe working conditions and excessive working hours.

These conditions can make migrant workers vulnerable to exploitation and discrimination. The Convention does not sufficiently address issues related to *discrimination in employment* and access to services, which can make migrants vulnerable to exploitation and discrimination. Employers can take advantage of the vulnerable situation of migrant workers to hire them under precarious working conditions.

The Convention does not sufficiently address issues related to *the criminalization of migrants* , which can include the arrest and detention of illegal migrants, and which can make migrants vulnerable to exploitation and discrimination.

Illegal migrants are often excluded from legal systems of protection and redress. The Convention does not sufficiently address issues related to the deportation of immigrants to their country of origin. Deportations can make immigrants vulnerable to exploitation and *discrimination* , as they are often deported to countries where they have no support and where economic and social conditions are precarious.

II

It is important to remember that the 1954 Convention is not a tool to fight against modern slavery, for that we must put in place additional policies and strategies to effectively combat this phenomenon, work on the establishment of procedures for reporting and investigating cases of modern exploitation, assisting victims, and prosecuting and punishing the perpetrators of these crimes.

REFUGE STATUS.

The 1954 Convention for the Suppression of Trafficking in Persons and Modern Slavery does not contain specific provisions on refugee status. In contrast, the 1951 Convention relating to the Status of Refugees and its 1967 Protocol contain refugee provisions that may have an impact on modern slavery.

Articles of the Convention on the Status of Refugees deal with protection and asylum for people fleeing persecution in their country of origin.

However, *this does not cover people who migrate for economic reasons* or for reasons related to factors such as violence or climate change.

These people may be more vulnerable to modern exploitation, consequent modern slavery because they cannot benefit from protection and asylum.

The articles of the Convention on the Status of Refugees do not sufficiently address issues related to restrictive migration policies, which can make refugees vulnerable to exploitation by preventing them from obtaining valid residence documents and exposing them to the risk of human trafficking.

The articles of the Convention on the Status of Refugees do not sufficiently address issues related to discrimination in employment and access to services, which can make refugees vulnerable to exploitation and discrimination.

The 1990 Convention

The 1990 Convention on the Rights of Refugees and Migrants is an international treaty adopted by the International Organization for Migration (IOM) in 1990.

It aims to protect the rights of refugees and migrants, including people who migrate for economic reasons or linked to factors such as violence or climate change. This Convention defines the fundamental principles in terms of the rights of refugees and migrants, such as the right to non-discrimination, the right to humane treatment, the right to personal security, the right to decent housing and the right to access to education and health care.

It also aims to protect people from exploitation, human trafficking and abuse. Unfortunately, *this convention has not been ratified by a large number of countries* and does not benefit from an effective monitoring mechanism to ensure its implementation.

This means that it is not used as a legal basis to protect the rights of refugees and migrants in most countries. Recall that the 1990 Convention on the Rights of Refugees and Migrants is an important tool to protect the rights of refugees and migrants, but it is important to put in place complementary policies and strategies to protect migrants who migrate for economic reasons or related to factors such as violence or climate change.

The 1990 Convention on the Rights of Refugees and Migrants, although it aims to protect the rights of refugees and migrants, can contribute to the modern exploitation of migrants in several ways:

The Convention does not provide for effective monitoring mechanisms to ensure its implementation, which makes it difficult to ensure that employers respect health and safety standards, minimum wages and workers' rights.

It does not sufficiently address issues related to restrictive migration policies, which can make migrants vulnerable to exploitation by preventing them from obtaining valid residency papers and exposing them to the risks of human trafficking.

She does not sufficiently address issues related to **discrimination in employment** and access to services, which can make migrants vulnerable to exploitation and discrimination.

Employers can take advantage of the vulnerable situation of migrant workers to hire them under precarious working conditions.

It does not sufficiently address issues related to the criminalization of migrants , which can include the arrest and detention of illegal migrants, and which can make migrants vulnerable to exploitation and discrimination. Illegal migrants are often excluded from legal systems of protection and redress.

The 1951 Convention

The 1951 Convention relating to the Status of Refugees is an international treaty adopted by the United Nations (UN) which defines the fundamental principles for the protection of refugees.

It establishes the right of refugees to non-refoulement, which prohibits states from returning refugees to a country where they risk facing persecution. It also establishes the criteria for determining who is considered a refugee, that is, a person who has fled their country of origin because of the fear of persecution based on their race, religion, nationality, membership in a social group or political opinions.

The 1951 Convention relating to the Status of Refugees contributes to the modern exploitation of migrants in the following cases:

The criteria for determining who is considered a refugee are quite strict and *do not cover people who migrate for family reasons or for reasons related to factors* such as violence or climate change.

These people may be more vulnerable to modern exploitation because they cannot benefit from refugee protection.

The articles of the Convention on the Status of Refugees *do not sufficiently address issues related to restrictive migration policies* , which can make refugees vulnerable to exploitation by preventing them from obtaining valid residence documents and exposing them to the risks of human trafficking.

The articles of the Convention on the Status of Refugees *do not sufficiently address issues related to discrimination in employment* and access to services, which can make refugees vulnerable to exploitation and discrimination.

The 1951 Convention relating to the Status of Refugees may contribute to the modern exploitation of migrants *because of the limits it places* on defining who is considered a refugee.

Indeed, the criteria for determining who is considered a refugee are quite strict and do not cover people who migrate for economic reasons or for reasons related to factors such as violence or climate change. These people may be more vulnerable to modern slavery because they cannot benefit from refugee protection.

Social classes

Modern slavery does not only affect migrant workers, but also vulnerable people in society, such as children, women and the elderly. Modern forms of exploitation include human trafficking, forced labor, forced marriage, forced prostitution, and sexual exploitation.

Human trafficking is a growing phenomenon worldwide, mainly affecting women and children. Victims of human trafficking are often forced to work in inhumane conditions, subjected to physical and psychological violence, and deprived of their liberty. Forced marriage is also a form of modern slavery, which mainly affects girls and women.

Victims of forced marriage are subjected to physical and psychological violence and deprived of their liberty and their right to education. Forced prostitution is also a

form of modern slavery that primarily affects women and girls.

Victims of forced prostitution are subjected to physical and psychological violence, and deprived of their liberty and their right to education. Remember that the fight against modern slavery, the exploitation of human beings and the modern exploitation of vulnerable people is a collective responsibility, which requires the commitment of all actors in society.

The progress

Advances in Combating Modern Slavery. In the United States, the federal government has implemented several initiatives to combat modern slavery, including:

Trafficking in Human Beings Act Victims Protection Act) of 2000, which aims to protect victims of human trafficking and to prosecute traffickers. This law has been revised several times to strengthen penalties for traffickers and improve protection services for victims. The 2013 National Human Trafficking Hotline , which aims to coordinate federal, state, and local efforts to combat human trafficking. It also aims to educate employers and consumers about the risks of modern slavery. State Department's Office to Monitor and Combat Trafficking in Persons , which is responsible for coordinating international efforts to combat human trafficking.

The US Department of Labor has also implemented initiatives to combat modern slavery in supply chains and industries, including auditing workers' working conditions and raising awareness. employers at risk of modern slavery.

Additionally, **the US government** has also signed international agreements such as the United Nations Convention Against Transnational Organized Crime Related to Human Trafficking to strengthen international cooperation to combat modern slavery.

In the United Kingdom , the government has introduced the Modern Slavery Act 2015, which aims to protect victims of human trafficking and prosecute traffickers. It also created a post of Commissioner for Combating Human Trafficking to coordinate the government's efforts.

In Australia , the government has introduced the Criminal Code Amendment (Slavery, Slavery-like Conditions and People Trafficking) Act 1999, which criminalizes human trafficking and increases penalties for traffickers.

It also established a National Center for Combating Human Trafficking to coordinate government efforts.

In France , the government implemented the Human Trafficking Law (Loi pour la sécurité interne) of 2003, which criminalizes human trafficking and increases penalties for traffickers. It also created a national human trafficking observatory to assess the needs of victims and coordinate government efforts.

In Switzerland , the government implemented the Human Trafficking Act (Human Trafficking Protection Act) of 2016, which criminalizes human trafficking and increases penalties for traffickers.

It also established a National Center for Combating Human Trafficking to coordinate government efforts.

Despite the efforts of governments to combat modern slavery, much remains to be done to eradicate this scourge.

International organisations, NGOs and civil society actors continue to call for stronger action.

In Germany , the government has implemented the Human Trafficking Act (Gesetz zur Bekämpfung der Menschenhandel) of 2005, which criminalizes human trafficking and increases penalties for traffickers. It also established a National Center for Combating Human Trafficking to coordinate government efforts.

In Canada , the government implemented the Human Trafficking Act (Bill C-452) of 2013, which criminalizes human trafficking and increases penalties for traffickers.

It also established a National Center for Combating Human Trafficking to coordinate government efforts.

In Japan , the government has implemented the Act on Punishing Acts Related to Child Prostitution and Child Pornography , and the Protection of Children) of 1999, which criminalizes human trafficking and increases penalties for traffickers. It also established a National Center for Combating Human Trafficking to coordinate government efforts.

In Nigeria , the government has enacted the Trafficking in Persons (Prohibition) Law Enforcement and Administration Act of 2003, which criminalizes human trafficking and increases penalties for traffickers.

In South Africa , the government has put in place the Prevention and Combating of Trafficking in Persons Act. Act) of 2013, which criminalizes human trafficking and increases penalties for traffickers. It also established a National Center for Combating Human Trafficking to coordinate government efforts.

In Kenya , the government has put in place the Counter- Trafficking in Persons Act. Act) of 2010, which criminalizes human trafficking and increases penalties for traffickers.

It also established a National Center for Combating Human Trafficking to coordinate government efforts.

In Ghana , the government has put in place the Human Trafficking Act . Act) of 2005, which criminalizes human trafficking and increases penalties for traffickers.

It also established a National Center for Combating Human Trafficking to coordinate government efforts.

Much remains to be done to eradicate this scourge. International organisations, NGOs and civil society actors continue to call for stronger actions to end this form of modern violence and ensure that the rights of vulnerable people are respected and protected.

FALLING MASKS

In 2016, **Thailand** was classified as a high-risk country for human trafficking by the United States Department of State. Thai authorities have been accused of not doing enough to fight human trafficking and failing to protect victims.

In 2019, **Australia** was accused of not doing enough to protect victims of modern slavery on fruit and vegetable farms. Foreign workers have been accused of being exploited and not being protected by Australian laws.

In 2020, **the US government** was accused of not doing enough to protect victims of modern slavery on US farms.

Foreign farm workers have been accused of being exploited and unprotected by US laws.

In 2021, the Indian government was accused of not doing enough to protect victims of modern slavery in coal mines. Mining workers have been accused of being exploited and unprotected by Indian laws.

International organisations , NGOs and civil society actors continue to monitor the implementation of laws to ensure that they are respected and that they protect the rights of victims.

Canada. There is evidence that Canada is also involved in modern slavery. Although Canada has laws in place to protect victims of modern slavery, there have been

instances where these laws have not been sufficiently implemented or where victims have not been sufficiently protected.

In 2017, a report by the International Labor Organization (ILO) revealed that temporary foreign workers in Canada were victims of human trafficking and other forms of exploitation. Workers were subjected to harsh working conditions, unpaid wages and illegal wage deductions.

In 2019, a report by the Food and Agriculture Organization of the United Nations (FAO) found that temporary foreign agricultural workers were victims of human trafficking and other forms of exploitation.

Workers were subjected to harsh working conditions, unpaid wages and illegal wage deductions.

In 2020 , reports revealed that foreign domestic workers in Canada were victims of human trafficking and other forms of exploitation.

Workers were subjected to harsh working conditions, unpaid wages and illegal wage deductions.

It is important to note that these examples are not exhaustive and there are many other cases where foreign workers in Canada have been victims of modern slavery.

The fight:

A social and political scheme

There are several ways to fight exploitation and modern slavery, the measures must be both social and political.

Socially : Raise awareness of these issues and work to protect the rights of immigrants and asylum seekers. It is important to support organizations working to protect the rights of migrant workers and to combat human trafficking. It is also important to support help and support services for victims of modern exploitation, including mental health services and rehabilitation programs.

On the political level : Put in place policies that protect the rights of migrant workers and asylum seekers.

It is important to have procedures in place to report and investigate cases of modern exploitation, and to prosecute and punish slave employers.

It is also important to have programs in place to help migrants integrate into their new country, including giving them valid residency papers and providing services such as education and health.

It is important to put in place migration policies that protect the rights of migrants, including helping them obtain legal status, and providing them with services such as education and health. We must establish *effective international cooperation* to combat human trafficking and modern slavery, including by exchanging information on criminal networks, training law enforcement and magistrates, and strengthening repressive mechanisms.

In addition: Establish programs to assist victims of human trafficking and modern slavery, including providing rehabilitation services and assisting them to return to their countries of origin. **Employers.** Strengthen the protection of workers' rights, including ensuring that employers respect health and safety standards, minimum wages and workers' rights.

It is also important to have mechanisms in place to report and investigate cases .

On the economic level : Put in place policies that promote the creation of decent and well-paid jobs for migrants. This can include job training programs, tax incentives for employers who hire migrant workers, and programs to facilitate migrant workers' access to credit and financial services.

On the cultural level: To raise awareness of the importance of cultural diversity and to fight against stereotypes and prejudices with regard to migrants.

This can include awareness campaigns and education programs for young people, as well as initiatives to promote the stories and achievements of migrants.

At the international level: Work in cooperation with other countries to combat the modern exploitation of migrants, in particular by exchanging information on criminal networks, training law enforcement and magistrates, and strengthening mechanisms of repression.

It is also important to work with international organizations to protect the rights of migrants and to help countries of origin improve economic and social conditions to reduce forced migration.

It is everyone's responsibility. We must put in place a combination of social, economic, cultural and political measures to combat modern exploitation. The world has evolved and the forms of exploitation have also evolved. It is important to raise awareness of these issues, to protect the rights of migrant workers and to work in cooperation with other countries and international organizations to eliminate the underlying causes of forced migration and to help victims of modern exploitation. .

Put in place more inclusive and fair migration policies that protect the rights of migrants and reduce the risk of exploitation.

This can include regularization programs for people living in a country illegally, more effective asylum policies for refugees, and temporary work programs that protect the rights of migrant workers.

Strengthen mechanisms for the protection of migrants' rights at the national and international level. This can include setting up systems for whistleblowing and reporting cases of exploitation, creating protection programs for victims of human trafficking, and establishing redress mechanisms for migrant victims of trafficking. abuse.

Raise awareness among the general public and employers of the risks of exploitation of migrants and the means of preventing them. This can include information and awareness campaigns, training programs for employers on health and safety standards and minimum wages, and education programs for migrants on their rights and how to exercise them. to be worth.

Foster international cooperation to combat the modern exploitation of migrants. This may include the establishment of partnership programs between governments, international organizations, employers and migrant rights organizations to strengthen protection and redress mechanisms for migrants and to combat human trafficking..

Ratification and implementation of international conventions and protocols that protect the rights of refugees and migrants. These actions must be complementary and be implemented simultaneously to be effective in the fight against the modern exploitation of migrants.

The struggle: a social and political scheme

There are several ways to counter the modern exploitation of migrants, which can include both social and political measures.

Socially , it is important to raise awareness of these issues and to work to protect the rights of immigrants and asylum seekers. It is important to support organizations working to protect the rights of migrant workers.

Politically , it is important to put in place policies that protect the rights of migrant workers and asylum seekers. It is important to have procedures in place to report and investigate cases of modern exploitation, and to prosecute and punish slave employers.

It is also important to have programs in place to help migrants integrate into their new country, including giving them valid residency papers and providing services such as education and health.

It is important to put in place migration policies that protect the rights of migrants, including helping them obtain legal status, and providing them with services such as education and health.

It is also important to have programs in place to help migrants integrate into their new country, including giving them valid residency papers and providing services such as education and health.

It is also important to establish *effective international cooperation* to combat human trafficking and modern slavery, including by exchanging information on criminal networks, training law enforcement and magistrates.

Employers. It is important to strengthen the protection of workers' rights, in particular by ensuring that employers respect health and safety standards, minimum wages and workers' rights. It is also important to have mechanisms in place to report and investigate cases .

It is important to put in place policies to protect the rights of migrant workers and to raise awareness among employers and consumers of the risks of modern exploitation of migrants.

Employers must adhere to health and safety standards, minimum wages and legal working hours to protect migrant workers from exploitation.

On the economic level , it is important to put in place policies that promote the creation of decent and well-paid jobs for migrants.

On the cultural level , it is important to raise awareness of the importance of cultural diversity and to combat stereotypes and prejudices against migrants.

This can include awareness campaigns and education programs for young people, as well as initiatives to promote the stories and achievements of migrants.

On the international level , it is important to work in cooperation with other countries to combat the modern exploitation of migrants, in particular by exchanging information on criminal networks, training law enforcement and magistrates, and by strengthening the mechanisms of repression.

It is important to have policies and programs in place to protect the vulnerable in society from modern exploitation. It is also important to educate employers and consumers about the risks of modern exploitation of vulnerable people and to put policies in place to protect the rights of vulnerable people.

Employers must adhere to health and safety standards, minimum wages and legal working hours to protect vulnerable people from exploitation.

It is important to strengthen mechanisms for the protection of the rights of vulnerable people at the national and international level to combat modern exploitation.

This may include the establishment of partnership programs between governments, international organizations, employers and vulnerable people's rights organizations to strengthen protection and redress mechanisms for vulnerable people and to combat human trafficking. Human being.

It is also important to set up awareness programs for young girls and women, so that they are informed of the risks of modern exploitation and the means of protecting themselves. It is important to strengthen child protection, education, health and justice systems for vulnerable people, to help them overcome abuse and trauma.

It is also important to set up research programs to understand the underlying causes of modern exploitation of vulnerable people and to develop effective solutions to address them. It is important to work closely with organizations defending the rights of vulnerable people and women's rights organizations to develop effective and sustainable solutions to combat the modern exploitation of vulnerable people.

It is everyone's responsibility. We must put in place a combination of social, economic, cultural and political measures to combat the modern exploitation of migrants.

It is important to raise awareness of these issues, to protect the rights of migrant workers and to work in cooperation with other countries and international organizations to eliminate the underlying causes of forced migration and to help victims of modern exploitation. .

ABOUT THE AUTHOR

Born in Togo in 1987, Kossi Ntiafalali Aziagba is considered the pillar of a silent immigrant revolution aimed at ending what he calls "modern slavery". As an immigrant himself, he denounces the torture and autocracy of African leaders, especially in his country of origin. He denounces the mistreatment of immigrants and asylum seekers, censorships and the use of refugee camps as a new channel for the exploitation of migrants and black people.

CONTACT THE AUTHOR:

Email: aziagba@gmail.com

Editor: ko6@aziagba.com

Reference Author: www.aziagba.com